100
THINGS TO DO IN
CHATTANOOGA
BEFORE YOU
DIE

100
THINGS TO DO IN
CHATTANOOGA
BEFORE YOU
DIE

2nd Edition

• •

ALEXI RUTH ENGESATH

REEDY PRESS

Library of Congress Control Number: 2018940103

ISBN: 9781681061597

Design by Jill Halpin

Printed in the United States of America
18 19 20 21 22   5 4 3 2 1

Please note that websites, phone numbers, addresses, and company names are subject to change or cancellation. We did our best to relay the most accurate information available, but due to circumstances beyond our control, please do not hold us liable for misinformation. When exploring new destinations, please do your homework before you go.

DEDICATION

For Adam, Trinity, Destiny, and Liberty

Let's go on an adventure!

CONTENTS

• •

Music and Entertainment

• •

Shopping and Fashion

INTRODUCTION

On its surface, Chattanooga is a small town with big charm. But dig a little deeper and you'll find a storied city, with a proud community and a complicated past. From its first known settlers, Chattanooga has been reinventing, reimagining, and rebuilding itself every few generations. For the last decade I've been digging into these stories to understand the culture and history of my adopted hometown.

In 1969 Walter Cronkite declared Chattanooga to be America's dirtiest city. Locals hate talking about Chattanooga's past pollution problems. They practically cringe at the mention of Cronkite's name, but understanding this bit of history is pivotal to appreciating the city's most recent transformation. From the dirtiest city in America to the Best Town Ever (Outsideonline.com/2008956/why-chattanooga-best-town-ever) in less than fifty years is quite a turnaround. The city of Chattanooga worked hard to clean up its act. By embracing its outdoorsy vibe, making space for the arts, and honoring its history, Chattanooga changed its reputation from the dirtiest city to the Scenic City.

This book is a love letter to Chattanooga.

My home. The best town ever.

• •

ACKNOWLEDGMENTS

This book simply would not have been possible without the infinite patience and support of dozens of people. First, many thanks to Molly Page, who dreams bigger for me than I do for myself. You believed I could do this, and the book you're holding in your hands is the proof you were right (as usual).

Thank you, Josh Stevens and the crew at Reedy Press for offering me this opportunity and allowing me to share my passion for Chattanooga.

Many thanks to the bevy of people who helped me cultivate and edit my list, including Tiffany Porter, Lisa Cutler, Tobi Weldon, Lee Gates, Lex Lepley, and Kaylee Franco. Your passion and insights made this book much more interesting.

To my amazing crew of friends who cheer me on every day in life—Jenn Gervens, Amy Kouse, Candy Morgan, and Lydia Vine. I don't think I could get through the day without hearing your voices.

Emily Lapish, Rachel Gates, Katie Brown, and Shana Redenbaugh, thank you for exploring the city with me, listening to me stress, and being a constant source of kindness and encouragement! You are my people.

Many thanks for the beautiful pictures supplied by Nicole Manning of Show Me a Smile Photography and Emily Lapish of Emily Lapish Photography. You are amazing artists, and I am proud to call you friends.

Special thanks to Ellen Shelley, who spent a weekend holed up with me, polishing my grammar. Your red pen and ceaseless encouragement are invaluable to me.

Mom and Dad, my love of storytelling came from hours spent listening to you tell and retell our family folklore. That and the love of purple shoes.

To my family and those who might as well be family (I'm looking at you, Hannah Baker), you are my favorite people on the planet, hands down. Come to Chattanooga—I know at least 100 things we can do here!

To my darling daughters, Trinity, Destiny, and Liberty, you are my greatest adventure. I love you more than I could properly express in this limited space.

Finally, to my husband, Adam Engesath . . . we did it, baby. You are my partner and my rock. Thank you for pushing, encouraging, and continuing to believe that I could make this dream come true. You are my heart.

• •

FOOD AND DRINK

TAKE A *PASSEGGIARE* ALONG THE STREETS
OF THE BLUFF VIEW ART DISTRICT

Work up an appetite in the Bluff View Art District, where the "sit and stay a while" vibe of the South meets old-world class. Stroll cobblestone roads lined with historic homes, now converted into shops and galleries. For a relaxing and rustic dining experience, visit Tony's Pasta Shop and Trattoria. Don't be intimidated by the name; *trattoria* is just a fancy Italian way of saying "small restaurant." Tony's menu features large portions of delicious hand-cut pasta dishes. But be careful not to fill up on bread! Dessert next door at Rembrandt's Coffee House is a must! Relax on Rembrandt's garden patio, or take your coffee to go and explore the outdoor River Gallery Sculpture Garden just around the corner.

Tony's Pasta Shop and Trattoria
212 High St., 423-265-5033

Rembrandt's Coffee House
204 High St.

River Gallery Sculpture Garden
400 E. 2nd St.

BluffViewArtDistrict.com

JOIN THE
WHISKEY REBELLION
AT CHATTANOOGA WHISKEY
EXPERIMENTAL DISTILLERY

For nearly one hundred years, manufacturing liquor in Chattanooga was illegal. In 2011 local businessmen began questioning the confusing loopholes and legal double standards that allowed distilleries to operate in other parts of the state (like the famous Jack Daniels Distillery, operating since the 1950s) while denying Chattanooga the same privilege. Rather than bootlegging like their Prohibition-era predecessors, they lobbied to change the law. Thus the Vote Whiskey Kickstarter movement was born. The campaign resulted in a bill lifting the antiquated restrictions and the opening of Chattanooga's first legal distillery in almost a century. Tour the Chattanooga Whiskey Experimental Distillery and sample the award-winning bourbons that changed the course of Chattanooga history. As any whiskey lover will tell you, good things come to those who wait.

1439 Market St., 423-760-4333
ChattanoogaWhiskey.com

WHO WILL WIN THE BATTLE
OF THE BURGER IN SOUTHSIDE?

In Southside the battle for best burger is brewing, and in this battle everyone wins. For the best bitty burger, Slick's 2.5-ounce baby burger packs in the flavor of a patty twice its size, while still leaving room for dessert. Discerning palates head to Main Street Meats for the best gourmet option. Topped with caramelized onions and gruyere cheese, the proper way to eat the local beef burger is with pinkies out. Vegetarians won't be left out of the fun. Terminal Brewhouse has the best burger alternative. The black bean burger will satisfy cravings, while maintaining a vegetarian's feeling of moral superiority. For the biggest mamma jamma, try Stir's double-patty Tillamook cheeseburger. But chew carefully, because this enormous burger just might dislocate your jaw.

Slicks
309 E. Main St., 423-760-4878

Terminal Brewhouse
1464 Market St., 423-752-8090
TerminalBrewhouse.com

Main Street Meats
217 E. Main St., 423-602-9568
MainStreetMeatsChatt.com

Stir
1444 Market St., 423-531-7847
StirChattanooga.com

AND THE WINNER IS ...
URBAN STACK!

For the most unique burgering experience in Southside—nay, in Chattanooga—there is no competition. Unconventional toppings and heaping patties at Urban Stack elevate the simple hamburger to an outstanding culinary experience. Garnished with unexpected ingredients like peppercorn bologna, pickled jalapeno, fried salami, chili, and cherry pepper relish, each bite takes your taste buds on a flavorful adventure. Special mention for the Steakhouse Burger—topped with BBQ sauce, bacon, onion rings, and atomic horsey sauce. The actual components of the atomic horsey sauce haven't been divulged, but it can be assumed that the secret ingredient is pure magic.

12 W. 13th St., 423-475-5350
UrbanStack.com

GET CRAFTY
AT THE SOUTHERN BREWERS FESTIVAL

Over the last decade the craft beer scene has exploded in Chattanooga, with local breweries popping up all around the city. To sample a wide variety of these creative and innovative lagers, pilsners, ales, and IPAs, buy a ticket for the Southern Brewers Festival, held at Ross's Landing. For more than twenty years, this summer festival has hosted dozens of local brewers as well as many nationally popular brands. The festival includes live music and food trucks and an adults-only VIP party on the pier.

201 Riverfront Pkwy.
SouthernBrewersFestival.com

NO STRETCHY PANTS OR HELMETS REQUIRED
ON PINTS AND PEDALS

For a unique pub crawl, take a guided tour with Pints and Pedals, stopping at some of the most popular bars in Southside and downtown. The fifteen-passenger cart is powered by the passengers pedaling in an oddly fun combination of a party bus and a spin class. Pick out three to five stops for the two-hour guided tour. Riders on the Pints and Pedals tour must be over twenty-one, so be sure to bring along a valid ID.

PintsandPedalstn.com

CELEBRATE THE LUCK OF THE 'NOOGANS
AT ST. PADDY'S DAY

Don't end up in a pinch. Instead, get decked out in green and spend St. Patrick's Day at the Party on the Parkway. The block party takes over Patten Parkway, with live music, food trucks, and family-friendly activities. The ticket proceeds are donated to charity, and kids under twelve can join the fun for free!

Looking for a more grown-up party? Head into the Honest Pint Irish pub, where celebrating the Irish is more than drinking green beer. Feast on the Irish/American cuisine, and enjoy the live Celtic music punctuating the festive mood.

But there's more fun to be had! Shut down the town on a St. Paddy's Day pub crawl with the St. Chatty's Day Double-Decker Bus Tour.

The Honest Pint
35 Patten Pkwy., 423-468-4192
TheHonestPint.com

Chattanooga Double Decker
423-226-1217
ChattanoogaDoubleDecker.com

DISCOVER YOUR BRUNCHING STYLE
WITH A CHATTANOOGA BRUNCH GUIDE

Is there anything more quintessentially Southern than Sunday Brunch? And Chattanoogans know how to brunch it up right. Looking for an excuse to day drink? Enjoy a boozy brunch at The Bitter Alibi, where classic brunch cocktails are elevated to a high art form. Each drink pairs beautifully with the traditional brunch menu (French toast and eggs), as well as the mouth-meltingly spicy Korean-inspired dishes. Feeling fancy? Put on your Sunday best for a bougie brunch at Easy Bistro. The upscale atmosphere and beautifully plated breakfast favorites turn brunching into an experience. Be forewarned: the eggs benedict might just change your life. Budget brunchers need not fear; Bluegrass Grill's down-home cooking will fill stomachs without completely emptying wallets. Get heaping helpings of traditional Southern fare, including savory grits and biscuits and gravy that rival grandma's best.

Bitter Alibi
825 Houston St., 423-362-5070
thebitteralibi.com

Easy Bistro
203 Broad St., 423-266-1121
EasyBistro.com

Bluegrass Grill
55 E Main St., 423-752-4020
Bluegrassgrillchattanooga.com

GRAB A DOLLAR TACO (OR TEN)
AT MOJO BURRITO

Mojo Burrito started out as a small Tex-Mex joint on a side street in St. Elmo. It has since grown into an immensely popular local chain with locations in East Brainerd, Red Bank, and a much larger, revamped space in St. Elmo. The menu features classic Tex-Mex favorites made to order with fresh ingredients and vegan/vegetarian-friendly options. The restaurant's campy vibe is complemented by the work of local artists displayed on the vibrantly colored walls. Get the most bang for your buck on Dollar Taco Day, when tacos are just a dollar. Each location has its own Dollar Taco Day, which means each week there are four chances to partake!

Red Bank
1800 Dayton Blvd., 423-870-6656
MojoBurrito.com

East Brainerd
1414 Jenkins Rd., 423-296-6656

St. Elmo
3950 Tennessee Ave., 423-822-6656

Ooltewah
9447 Brandmore Ln., 423-531-6656

BRUNCH WITH THE PUNKS
AT ARETHA FRANKENSTEINS

Aretha Frankensteins looks like just another suburban cottage tucked away in a quiet North Shore neighborhood. Inside, however, beats the heart of a punk rock cafe. This is not your typical Southern Sunday brunch place. Framed vintage cereal boxes and obscure band posters line the walls, while a skateboarding skeleton chandelier dangles overhead. The dining room is tiny and usually packed. But the crowd waiting on the porch hasn't gathered for the ambience or quick service; they've come for the pancakes. Roughly the size of a dinner plate, the short stack is like biting into a cloud. The menu also features no-frills breakfast classics like crispy bacon, waffles, and omelettes served in heaping portions. Not a fan of waiting? Grab a box of Aretha's pancake mix and whip up a batch at home.

518 Tremont St., 423-265-7685
Arethas.com

FEED YOUR CAFFEINE ADDICTION
AND YOUR SOUL

How do you transform a city into a community? One cup of coffee at a time. Gather with community leaders empaneled at The Camp House to discuss topics varying from theology to city planning. At Mad Priest Coffee Roasters the mantra is "Craft excellent coffee. Educate the curious. Champion the displaced." Mad Priest lives up to those lofty goals by employing refugees resettled in Chattanooga, as well as regularly hosting community events to educate the community on how to embrace the displaced. Or, to more directly perk up someone's day, order a $2 "pay it forward" at Cadence Coffee House and provide a cup of hot coffee to someone who may not be able to afford it.

The Camp House
149 E. Martin Luther King, Blvd., 423-702-8081

thecamphouse.com

Mad Priest Coffee Roasters
1900 Broad St., Suite C, 423-393-3834

Madpriestcoffee.com

Cadence Coffee Company
11 E. 7th St., 423-521-7686

CadenceCoffeeCo.com

CRAM YOUR GULLET FULL
OF CHAMPY'S WORLD-FAMOUS CHICKEN

Champy's World-Famous Chicken takes a no-frills approach to Southern cuisine. The food is piled high on Styrofoam plates, and rolls of paper towels adorn every table. Champy's has a ramshackle "good ol' boys" feel, with graffitied dollar bills and expired license plates lining the walls and sports on every screen. Their simple menu includes Southern favorites like hand-breaded fried chicken, hot tamales, fried green tomatoes, and homemade key lime pie so good it'll make you wanna slap your mama.* For a laid-back atmosphere and good cheap eats, Champy's might just be your cup of (sweet) tea.

6925 Lee Hwy.
526 E. MLK Blvd.
423-752-9198
ChampysChicken.com

*"So good it'll make you wanna slap your mama" is a Southern colloquialism. No actual mamas will be harmed in the consumption of Champy's key lime pie.

IT'S A GOOD DAY FOR GOOD DOG!

North Shore's Good Dog is daily dishing up the best hot dogs in Chattanooga. All-beef hot dogs, bratwurst, and a wide variety of homemade sausages, as well as vegetarian options, guarantee there's a dog for everyone. The menu offers creative flavor combinations, each bun overflowing with delicious toppings. To get the perfect dog, order from the Build Your Own menu. Choose from unconventional toppings like sriracha aioli, lime cream, and poached eggs, or stick to classics like chili and sauerkraut. Wondering why there are holes in the table? They are specially designed to hold the frites, which are hand-cut fries served in paper cones. The friendly staff, fresh food, and funky vibe are sure to make anyone a dog lover.

34 Frazier Ave., 423-475-6175
EatAtGoodDog.com

START THE DAY SWEET
AT JULIE DARLING'S

There's no better way to start the day than with a donut from Julie Darling's. Try their best-selling pancake and bacon donut. This sweet and savory treat combines all the best breakfast foods in one surprisingly delicious bite.

121 Frazier Ave., 423-591-3737
JDDonuts.com

CAN'T STAND THE HEAT?
GET A COOL TREAT AT CLUMPIES

Clumpies has been a staple on Frazier Avenue since 1999 and has expanded with locations in St. Elmo, Lookout Mountain, and Southside. Their wildly popular gourmet ice cream is an indulgent summer treat. The secret to Clumpies' delicious concoctions is producing the ice cream in small batches with fresh ingredients. Each bite is bursting with flavor. The freezer is packed with dozens of classic favorites as well as a few seasonal surprises. Feeling overwhelmed by the choices? Try a few samples before settling on a flavor. Whether it's scooped into a waffle cone, mixed into a shake, or smothered in chocolate sauce as a sundae, satisfaction is guaranteed.

North Shore
26 Frazier Ave., 423-267-5425
Clumpies.com

St. Elmo
3917 St. Elmo Ave., 423-821-0807

Lookout Mountain
1110 E. Brow Rd., 423-708-7531

Southside
1401 Market St. 423-648-5425

TAKE THE LONG, STRANGE (AND DELICIOUS) TRIP
TO THE YELLOW DELI

The Yellow Deli could best be described as a bizarro mash-up of a log cabin and a hippy commune. The sounds of bluegrass music and the smell of baking bread waft through the air, sharply contrasted by trippy, kaleidoscopic murals covering the walls. The deli is operated by the unorthodox Twelve Tribes, whose religious views are scrawled on the walls as well as in pamphlets around the deli. While the legitimacy of the Twelve Tribes is hotly contested around Chattanooga, the quality of the food at the Yellow Deli is not. The menu consists of deli standards served on homemade breads in heaping portions. The vibe is odd but not off-putting. The hours, like everything else about the deli, are a little weird; they're open 24/5 (Sunday at noon to Friday at 3 p.m.).

737 McCallie Ave., 423-468-1777
YellowDeli.com/chattanooga

NO NEED FOR THE NEWFANGLED,
GET OLD-FASHIONED BBQ AT SUGAR'S RIBS

Nestled on the side of Missionary Ridge, Sugar's Ribs is dishing up old-fashioned roadside BBQ with a breathtaking view. Step up to the counter and try not to be distracted by the heavenly smells coming from the kitchen. Ribs are a great choice of course, but for something a little unconventional try the crispy potato nachos with brisket. The meat is slow roasted and juicy on the inside, with a little crunch on the outside. Macaroni, Texas pintos, and cornbread complement the sweet and tangy BBQ perfectly. Grab a seat on the porch near the railing for an unobstructed view of the mountains surrounding Chattanooga. Don't worry about getting messy. At the end of the meal Sugar's provides warm damp towels to get hands and faces sauce-free.

2450 15th Ave., 423-826-1199
SugarsRibs.com

THERE'S ROOM FOR ONE MORE
AT ONE TABLE

The nonprofit organization Causeway is working to break down barriers in Chattanooga by inviting the entire city to a pre-Thanksgiving potluck, bringing everyone together to sit down together at one table. The mission of this annual One Table event is to connect neighbors and communities, and open up communication. The potluck takes place on MLK Boulevard the Monday before Thanksgiving, and the meal is absolutely free. The main dishes are donated by local restaurants; just bring along a side dish or dessert to share. Hundreds sit down together, to break bread and give thanks. When you sit at One Table, it's an opportunity to meet someone new, to hear their stories, to see the city through someone else's eyes. There's always room for one more at the table.

MLK Blvd. between Miller Park and Miller Plaza
Causeway.org/onetable

BLOW OUT YOUR BIRTHDAY CANDLES
AT BOCCACCIA RISTORANTE ITALIANO

Tucked away in a quiet corner of the Southern Saddlery Building, Boccaccia Ristorante Italiano is an upscale eatery with a cozy, rustic setting. Rustic wood tables and low lighting create a romantic atmosphere, perfect for special occasions. In fact, those who spend their birthday at Boccaccia get the ultimate gift, free pasta and dessert (bring along a dinner companion and an ID, as both are required). The food is almost too beautiful to eat. Almost. With house specials like agnello alle erbe (lamb chops) and classics like cappellini pomodoro, lasagna, and ravioli, there's no wrong way to order. For a sweet finish, dessert is a must. Boccaccia will provide a birthday candle, though after that meal it might be difficult to come up with a wish.

3077 Broad St., 423-266-2930
BoccacciaRestaurant.com

GET A BITE OF THE BAYOU
AT BOATHOUSE ROTISSERIE
AND RAW BAR

Just off the Riverpark (see page 53), the Boathouse Rotisserie and Raw Bar is daily dishing up seafood with a Southern flair. The menu features bayou-inspired dishes like the spicy voodoo chicken and the shrimp po'boy, alongside freshly prepared seafood. The Boathouse is a bit expensive but worth the sticker price. For the best views of the river, request a seat out on the porch and enjoy a relaxing and romantic evening watching the sun set behind the mountains.

1459 Riverside Dr., 423-622-0122
BoathouseChattanooga.com

BUST OUT THE CHOPSTICKS
FOR ARTISANAL RAMEN AT TWO TEN JACK

The word *ramen* evokes images of slurping sodium-saturated noodles out of a microwavable cup, but at Two Ten Jack, it's not that kind of ramen. The dishes are authentic Japanese, with a touch of Southern flair. Along with ramen, the menu features small plates like crispy brussels and J.F.C. (Japanese Fried Chicken) that are sure to please Southern palates. Not sure what to get? Let the waiter serve as your culinary guide. Try the yakitori skewers or sushi. Though a Japanese-inspired gastropub serving artisanal ramen sounds fairly pretentious, Two Ten Jack has a casual vibe. Its location in the basement of Warehouse Row (see page 120) is an inviting environment to sit and share a meal. Just don't ask for a to-go box. Reheating ramen is a no-no!

1110 Market St., Suite FC4, 423-551-8799
TwoTenJack.com

SATISFY CURRY CRAVINGS
AT RAIN THAI BISTRO

Got a hankering for curry? Rain Thai Bistro has what you need. Get started with steamed dumplings and crispy spring rolls served with a tangy dipping sauce. The appetizers come in huge helpings, but they're so delicious it may be hard to share. The sushi menu has an abundance of fresh and flavorful rolls. Feeling adventurous? Ask the chef to make his favorite roll and see what comes out! But save room for the main course. There are dozens of dishes to choose from, but at Rain Thai it's all about the curry. For the perfect mix of tangy, spicy, and sweet, try the Rain Thai Curry. To get the most panang for your buck, come at lunchtime when the helpings are huge and the ticket price is small.

6933 Lee Hwy., Suite 400, 423-386-5586
RainThaiBistro.net

EXPERIENCE FOUR STAR CUISINE AT
ST. JOHN'S AND ST. JOHN'S MEETING PLACE

Like many of the buildings on Chattanooga's Southside, St. John's Restaurant is a testimony to the beauty of reclaiming history. The turn-of-the-century luxury hotel (once named St. John's) lay in ruins until being granted landmark status in the early '90s. Restored, reimagined, and revived, St. John's Restaurant pays homage to its opulent history with more than just its name. Expect a four-star dining experience unparalleled in the city, paired with a selection from their award-winning wine collection. Be sure to dress to impress. There may not be a written dress code, but those who arrive underdressed may be invited to dine next door at St. John's Meeting Place. Fortunately, Meeting Place shares its sister restaurant's commitment to quality (and extensive wine list) in a relaxed, flip-flop-friendly environment.

1278 Market St.
423-266-4400
Stjohnsrestaurant.com

DID YOU KNOW

St. John's (originally named the Ellis Hotel) was the work of famed Chattanooga architect R.H. Hunt, who designed the Solomon Federal Building, the Tivoli Theatre, and the Lookout Mountain Hotel (which is now a part of Covenant College), as well as dozens of other iconic Chattanooga buildings.

STUFF YOUR PIE HOLE
AT THE MOONPIE GENERAL STORE

Did you know that Chattanooga is the birthplace of MoonPies? The Chattanooga Bakery began manufacturing the classic Southern treat more than one hundred years ago. During the Depression, a MoonPie only cost a nickel and came to be known as the workingman's lunch. The marshmallow snack has only grown in popularity. The hometown delicacy even inspired country musician Big Bill Lister to write the honkey tonk classic "Gimme an RC Cola and a MoonPie." In the heart of downtown Chattanooga, the MoonPie General Store is dedicated to Chattanoogans' love of all things MoonPie. Get nostalgic playing with vintage toys, find a retro gift, and of course grab some RC Colas and MoonPies.

429 Broad St., 423-877-0592
MoonPie.com

GET A LITTLE ROWDY
AT HI-FI CLYDE'S ON MAIN

For a raucous good time, check out the Southside's most beloved neighborhood bar, Hi-Fi Clyde's on Main. The popular eatery features BBQ, burgers, and Southern-style fare in heaping portions, as well as strong cocktails, shots, and beer from local brewers. The garage-style patio doors pay homage to the previous owners, Clyde's Auto Glass Shop, whose name is still painted on the side of the building. Clyde's has all the charm of a rowdy honky tonk, without the risk of a drunken brawl. Live music and indoor Ping-Pong tables mean the noise level typically ranges from boisterous to a dull roar. Don't be surprised to see a line of people waiting outside. Clyde's is well-loved and well worth the wait.

122 W. Main St.
423-362-8335
Hificlydeschattanooga.com

MUSIC AND ENTERTAINMENT

GO CRUISN'
ON THE *SOUTHERN BELLE*

Take a relaxing ride down the Tennessee River on the *Southern Belle*. Daily sightseeing cruises last an hour and a half, passing under the bridges and by the old factories lining the banks of the river. The sightseeing cruise is a favorite field trip for local schools, but don't be deterred. The kids' enthusiasm can be infectious and can make for an even more entertaining ride. For a romantic evening, try a dinner or sunset cruise. The trip includes a buffet-style dinner, live music, and dancing. Watch the sun set behind the mountains, and let the lights of Chattanooga guide you back to the dock at twilight. Expect calm waters, cool breezes, and dazzling views of the river.

201 Riverfront Pkwy., 423-266-4488
ChattanoogaRiverboat.com

TIP
This Valentine's Day give your sweetheart an extra-special gift with a Be Mine Cruise. Watch the sunset together on the evening cruise, then dance the night away. The tickets include a buffet dinner, champagne served in souvenir glasses, and a keepsake photo.

GET DAZZLED
BY THE JEWEL OF THE SOUTH

In its heyday, the Tivoli Theatre was nicknamed "the Jewel of
the South." The flashing marquee, gold-domed ceiling, crystal
chandeliers, and plush red velvet seats harken back to the grand
old days of theatergoing. The space is undeniably charming, but
there are a few vintage quirks. The seats are fairly close together,
so be prepared to get up close and personal with your neighbor.
Also, the bathrooms are beautiful, but there aren't a lot of stalls,
so expect a wait. The Tivoli regularly draws popular musicians
and comedians, as well as touring Broadway shows, and it serves
as the home of the Chattanooga Symphony and Opera (see page
36). Take in a show, and see why the Tivoli is still a Chattanooga
treasure.

709 Broad St., 423-757-5580
TivoliChattanooga.com

START THE CHRISTMAS SEASON
WITH A BELOVED HOLIDAY TRADITION, *THE NUTCRACKER*

Hum along to the familiar melodies of Tchaikovsky and be spellbound by Clara's fevered Christmas dream in *The Nutcracker*. The Nutcracker Prince, Mouse King, and Sugar Plum Fairy are beautifully brought to life by the Chattanooga Ballet, with accompaniment by the Chattanooga Symphony Orchestra (see page 36). *The Nutcracker* is performed annually at the Tivoli Theatre (see page 33), and the grand theater provides a regal backdrop for the holiday ballet.

Tivoli Theatre
709 Broad St., 423-757-5580

Chattanooga Ballet
ChattanoogaBallet.net

HURRAY FOR THE RED, WHITE, AND BLUE!
CELEBRATE AMERICA'S BIRTHDAY AT POPS ON THE RIVER

Pack a picnic lunch, grab the lawn chairs, and don't forget the sparklers. It's time for Chattanooga's annual Independence Day celebration! On July 3 enjoy a free concert in Coolidge Park (see page 87), courtesy of the Chattanooga Symphony Orchestra. While waiting for the main event at dusk, join in a show tunes sing-along. The grand finale is a fireworks spectacular over the Tennessee River, accompanied by the symphony (see page 36) playing patriotic standards. Pops on the River is a local favorite. For decent parking and a good seat, come early. Not a fan of crowds? Several perches along three downtown bridges offer great views of the fireworks with a bit more elbow room.

150 River St., 423-643-5956
ChattanoogaPops.com

LET WORLD-CLASS MUSICIANS BRING THE ARTS TO YOU
WITH THE CSO IN THE COMMUNITY

The Chattanooga Symphony & Opera (CSO) brings classical music to the community, with free concerts around Chattanooga throughout the year. Pack a sack lunch and catch an afternoon show at Warehouse Row (see page 120), which regularly hosts the CSO in a lunchtime series. For those who have sensory sensitivities, the CSO presents a special-needs concert each month. The sensory-friendly concerts invite attendees to move and get close to the musicians, and a quiet room is provided in case of overstimulation. Bring the whole family along for the Veterans Day Concert, held annually at the Soldiers and Sailors Memorial Auditorium.

Chattanooga Symphony & Opera
ChattanoogaSymphony.org

GET WEIRD
AT MAINX24

Each year the Southside community hosts Mainx24, a twenty-four-hour street festival, and the whole city is invited to the party. Start with a pancake breakfast at the firehouse, where all proceeds and donations benefit local schools. Join the crowd lining Main Street for the haphazard, almost wild, Christmas parade. The Mainx24 block party is organized by the residents, businesses, and community of Southside as a labor of love. There are one hundred events throughout the twenty-four-hour period. Be forewarned, things can get weird. Just go with it! Past events included Christmas caroling, fashion shows, sumo wrestling, human foosball, live art demonstrations, and themed dance parties.

Mainx24.com

GET ACQUAINTED WITH THE BIG NINE AND CHATTANOOGA'S JAZZ HISTORY
COURTESY OF JAZZANOOGA

A century ago, the 9th Street District (now MLK Boulevard) was a thriving community and hub for black entrepreneurship. Known as the Big Nine, the district was a hotbed of juke joints playing jazz and blues. It was the birthplace of legendary blues singer Bessie Smith and Grammy Award–winning jazz musician Yusef Lateef. Today Jazzanooga sits squarely in the old Big Nine district and strives to preserve the history and culture of jazz in Chattanooga. With community education, open jam sessions, and amazing performances, Jazzanooga is inspiring the next generation of jazz lovers. Celebrate Chattanooga's rich musical history during Jazz Appreciation Month (JAM) in April. Each year Chattanooga hosts JAMfest, with pop-up concerts featuring local artists. Visit Jazzanooga's website for a schedule of events.

431 E. MLK Blvd.
423-402-0452
Jazzanooga.org

CELEBRATE MEXICO'S VICTORY OVER THE FRENCH
AT THE RUNNING OF THE CHIHUAHUAS

Celebrate Cinco de Mayo Chattanooga style, with Hits 96's annual Running of the Chihuahuas. The First Tennessee Pavilion is transformed into a mini racetrack, where more than a hundred Chihuahuas will compete for fame, glory, and a small plaque. The family friendly event kicks off with live music and DJs to get the racers pumped for the main event. The dogs run in heats, competing for the big enchilada—the final race. The Running of the Chihuahuas is Chattanooga's largest Cinco de Mayo celebration, but the festivities may not actually fall on May 5. The party takes place every year on a Saturday; to confirm party details, visit Hits96.com/categories/events.

A THRILLING START TO SUMMER
BEGINS AT LAKE WINNIE

For more than ninety years, the opening of Lake Winnepesaukah Amusement Park has signaled the official beginning of summer. The small park has a handful of medium-sized coasters and those spinning carnival-style rides whose sole purpose seems to be to induce nausea. The park also has plenty of kid-friendly family favorites like the Ferris wheel, paddle boats, the carousel, and bumper cars. Keep heat stroke at bay in the Soak Ya Water Park. Grab an inflatable tube and take a leisurely float around the lazy river, plunge down waterslides, and let the little ones run wild in the kid-safe waterworks. If the rides aren't exciting enough, visit during Halloween when the park transforms into Lake WinnepeSPOOKah, designed to scare and delight thrill seekers of every age.

1730 Lakeview Dr., Rossville, GA, 706-866-5681
LakeWinnie.com

TAKE IN A MOVIE UNDER THE STARS
AT THE WILDERNESS OUTDOOR MOVIE THEATER

For the price of less than one movie ticket, catch a double feature at the Wilderness Outdoor Movie Theater. The drive-in sits just over the Georgia border in the middle of nowhere, far from city lights. Come when the gates open to snag a prime parking spot. Kill time before the movie starts in the fields surrounding the theater, ideal for tossing a football or Frisbee. Enjoy a dazzling pre-show as the sun sets behind the mountains and the stars take over the sky. Outside food is not permitted, but the concession stand is stocked with more than the standard popcorn and soda. Grab a funnel cake, snuggle under a blanket, and settle in for an unparalleled movie experience.

217 Old Hales Gap Rd., Trenton, GA, 706-657-8411
WildernessTheater.com

HAVE A TOE TAPPIN',
KNEE SLAPPIN', HAND CLAPPIN'
GOOD TIME AT THE 3 SISTERS
BLUEGRASS FESTIVAL

Held annually at Ross's Landing, the 3 Sisters Bluegrass Festival celebrates traditional and contemporary bluegrass, with a lineup of beloved local musicians as well as bigger names in the genre. The concerts are free and incredibly popular, so parking downtown can be a bit of a challenge. Once you've snagged a spot, spread a blanket and settle in. Breathe in the crisp air and drink in music inspired by Tennessee's mountains and rivers. Outside food and drinks are prohibited, but food trucks surrounding the festival will keep bellies full and bodies fueled for dancing.

Ross's Landing
3sistersbluegrass.com

ROCK OUT
AT THE RIVERBEND FESTIVAL

The Riverbend Festival has drawn thousands of music lovers to Ross's Landing for decades. The eight-day festival hosts one hundred artists on multiple stages, running the gamut of genres, from country and nostalgic one-hit wonders to Christian, rock, and blues. Because June is not an ideal time of year to have an outdoor anything in Tennessee, expect blistering heat and lots of humidity. There's little to no shade, so smart attendees bring water and umbrellas to stave off heat stroke. But concertgoers don't let the heat keep them down. Be ready to dance no matter how high the temperatures rise. Chattanoogans have mixed feelings about Riverbend and the traffic and trash it produces, but the fireworks finale closing out the festival more than makes up for the inconveniences.

200 Riverfront Pkwy.
RiverbendFestival.com

TIP
Take in the fireworks finale for free. Bring a lawn chair to Coolidge Park or the Market Street Bridge; both are ideal perches for watching the show while avoiding the hoards of concertgoers.

START A SUMMER TRADITION
WITH MOVIES IN THE PARK

These days, going to the movies can get crazy expensive, especially for families. Movies in the Park takes the pain out of going to the theater, with free family friendly movies. Watch a screening of popular kids movies at Coolidge Park (see page 87) each Saturday night in July. Get there early to stake out a good spot because the fun starts long before the sun goes down. Let the kids play in the fountains (see page 55) or ride bikes along the trails while waiting for the movie to begin. Bring along blankets, folding chairs, and a cooler filled with snacks and drinks. Forgot the popcorn? Don't fret! There are concession stands around the park. After dark, snuggle down for the main event. Start a great family tradition without breaking the bank.

150 River St.
FirstThingsFirst.org

LOOKING TO BEAT THE SUMMER HEAT?
JUST WAIT FOR NIGHTFALL

The Nightfall Concert Series takes over Miller Plaza and the surrounding blocks on Friday nights from May to August. The outdoor concert is a fixture of the downtown music scene; rain or shine the show goes on. Nightfall is characterized by diverse musicians from a wide range of genres, from indie to bluegrass, Southern rock to jazz. Market Street is shut down for motorcycle parking, and the adjacent block of MLK Boulevard is lined with food trucks and vendors. Leash your dogs and untether the kids; just don't forget the lawn chairs. Some folding chairs are provided near the stage, but they tend to fill up early. Speakers surrounding the plaza make every seat the best seat in the house.

Nightfall at Miller Plaza
850 Market St.
NightfallChattanooga.com

SPORTS AND RECREATION

DIVE INTO THE NEW YEAR
WITH LULA LAKE LAND TRUST'S POLAR PLUNGE

Start the New Year with a shock to the system at the annual Lula Lake Land Trust's Polar Plunge. Leap from a boulder into the near-freezing water and prepare for what one plunger described as the "longest 15 foot swim of my life." Feeling brave? Zip line to the middle of the lake and try to make it to shore before hypothermia sets in. Tickets include all-you-can-eat chili, as well as hot chocolate, bloody marys, and spiked hot cider, which are sure to get the blood pumping back to those frozen extremities. All proceeds from ticket sales and donations support the Lula Lake Land Trust for the continued preservation of the 8,000-acre watershed.

5000 Lula Lake Rd., Lookout Mountain, GA
706-820-0520
For maps of Lula Lake, visit: Lulalake.org/find-us-maps-directions/trail-maps/

ROOT, ROOT, ROOT FOR THE HOME TEAM
AT AT&T FIELD

Summer just isn't summer without baseball. Head to AT&T Field in the heart of downtown to cheer the Chattanooga Lookouts to victory. The relaxed, noisy vibe is perfect for kids. But if the game isn't enough to keep them occupied, team mascot Looie the Lookout and a DJ provide a bit of extra entertainment. Fans are invited to compete for free T-shirts and other prizes by participating in silly games and races. The small stadium has little to no shade, so use generous amounts of sunscreen and wear a cap. With a hot dog in one hand and a soda in the other, there's no better way to spend a summer day.

AT&T Field
201 Power Alley

TIP
The most popular game of the year is Used Car Night. Local dealerships donate used cars, which are then given away each inning. To enter the drawing, bring along a valid license and fill out the entry form at the gate. Be sure to get tickets early, as this game sells out every year.

TAKE A WILD RIDE
DOWN THE OCOEE RIVER RAPIDS

During the 1996 Olympics, the Ocoee River hosted the world's first whitewater event held on a natural river. The Class III and IV rapids drew the best of the best to compete with kayaks and canoes, but the Ocoee River isn't just for Olympians. Each year it draws whitewater enthusiasts of every skill level to feel the rush of its rapids. Whether tubing, whitewater rafting, or kayaking, there's an adventure for just about everyone. The Ocoee River is controlled by the dam, which means the full course is only watered during the summers. Be sure to check the Tennessee Valley Authority's schedule to guarantee the most exciting ride on the river.

TVA.gov

TEST YOUR METTLE
IN CHATTANOOGA'S IRONMAN

The participants in Chattanooga's Ironman spend years training to win a lifetime of bragging rights. The grueling course takes athletes on a 2.4-mile downstream swim in the Tennessee River, 116-mile bike ride around the Tennessee and Georgia countryside, and then a run around downtown for a total distance of 26.2 miles. Each year thousands of the nation's top athletes compete in the event, pushing themselves to improve their times and stamina. The course takes anywhere from ten to sixteen hours after plunging into the river, and finishing is truly an amazing feat. Not interested in the rigorous training to become a triathlete? Be a spectator and root for the racers by offering sweaty high fives and enthusiastic cheers as they cross the finish line at Ross's Landing to become ironmen.

Ironman.com/triathlon/events/americas/ironman/
chattanooga.aspx#/axzz4Oa0skQ1l

TAKE A SCENIC STROLL
ALONG THE TENNESSEE
RIVERPARK TRAIL

Looking for a less rugged outdoor experience? The Tennessee
Riverpark, which locals call the Riverwalk, has wide, well-paved
paths winding alongside the Tennessee River. Beginning at the
Chickamauga Dam and stretching more than eight miles to Ross's
Landing (see page 94) in downtown Chattanooga, the Riverpark is
perfect for joggers and bikers of every skill level. Keep track of how
far you've traveled with the bronze fish embedded in the sidewalk
marking each half mile of the trail. The Riverpark also features
outdoor artwork (see page 101), fishing piers, boat launches, a
playground (see page 83), and dozens of picnic tables and shelters.
For night owls, the path is well lit and open twenty-four hours a day.
But please leave your pooch at home, as dogs are not allowed at the
Riverpark.

Tennessee Riverpark
4301 Amnicola Hwy. (just one of many entrances to the park)
HamiltonTN.gov/tnriverpark

LEAVE NO STONE UNTURNED
IN THE RACCOON MOUNTAIN CAVERNS

The Raccoon Mountain Caverns were first explored by Leo Lambert, who famously discovered Ruby Falls (see page 91). While excavating, Lambert unearthed a large room of formations he named the Crystal Palace. With an eye toward commercialization, Lambert expanded the trails and named the cave system the Tennessee Caverns. Today the Crystal Palace guided tour is a forty-five-minute expedition along lighted pathways through beautiful formations. For something a bit more rigorous, take a wild cave tour through the five-and-a-half-mile network of underground tunnels. Get down and dirty as you belly crawl through the undeveloped cave systems. Gloves, knee pads, and lighted helmets are required (and provided) for safety. For a real challenge, take the Waterfall Dome Expedition, which lasts about four hours and leads to a seventy-five-foot underground waterfall.

319 W. Hills Dr.
RaccoonMountain.com

MAKE A SPLASH
IN CHATTANOOGA'S FREE OUTDOOR FOUNTAINS

Want a free way to keep kids cool on a hot summer day? Throw on a swimsuit and head to one of Chattanooga's free outdoor interactive waterworks. Downtown, just outside the aquarium, explore the Plaza and the Passage. The shallow water winds around the aquarium like a miniature version of the river it overlooks. The Passage wading pool is perfect for youngsters not yet able to swim but ready to make a splash. Across the river visit the Coolidge Park Play Fountain, which borrows its theme from the carousel housed a few steps away (see page 87). Elephants and horses spray water, while spires of water shoot up intermittently. The play is free, but the parking is not. Be sure to bring a few quarters for the meters.

Aquarium Fountains
1 Broad St.

Coolidge Park Fountains
150 River St.

CRUISE AMERICA'S LARGEST UNDERGROUND LAKE
AT THE LOST SEA ADVENTURE

Take a guided tour of the Lost Sea Caverns, whose colorful history is scrawled all over its walls. Graffiti documents the presence of the Cherokee, Civil War soldiers, moonshiners, and more than a few mischievous teens. Come prepared with a sweater and flashlight. The cave remains a brisk fifty-eight degrees year-round, and although there is low lighting, a flashlight gives a better view of the cave flowers and formations along the path. Follow the winding trail down to where glass-bottomed boats cruise the perimeter of the ethereal Lost Sea. While the walk down is fairly easy, the trip back up is a bit more of a challenge. With 25 percent less oxygen and steep inclines, there's no shame in taking a break on the benches provided.

140 Lost Sea Rd., Sweetwater, TN
423-337-6616
TheLostSea.com

THERE ARE PLENTY OF FISH
IN THE *SCENIC* CITY

Chattanooga boasts more species of freshwater fish in diverse habitats than anywhere in the United States. Cast a line in one of Chattanooga's rivers, streams, or lakes and find everything from freshwater trout to river monsters. Before wading in, be sure to obtain a fishing license, and be familiar with local policies regarding which fish can be kept and which need to be released. Sport fishermen can find gear, fishing guides, and expert advice at Blue Ridge Fly Fishing. Looking to snag a trophy fish? Charter a boat with Scenic City Fishing and cruise for record-breaking bass, crappie, and catfish, whose size and ferocity will require no embellishment.

Blue Ridge Fly Fishing
205 Manufacturers Rd., Suite 105
blueridgeflyfishing.com

ScenicCityFishing.com

CHEER LIKE A CHATTAHOOLIGAN
AT A CHATTANOOGA FOOTBALL CLUB MATCH

Grab a cowbell and join the rabid fans of the Chattanooga Football Club. The self-proclaimed Chattahooligans are almost as entertaining to watch as the match itself. Show up a little early to the home games and join the March to the Match as the Chattahooligans parade through the stadium to their own cheering section. Led by a drum line, oversized flags, and occasionally Darth Vader, the Chattahooligans definitely put the fan in fanatical. Throughout the match, they unabashedly support their team with catchy cheers and contagious enthusiasm. A word to the wise: I wouldn't use the "s" word in the stadium unless you want a long lecture about the proper, worldwide-accepted term for the sport. This is not soccer. This is Chattanooga football.

Finley Stadium
1826 Carter St.
ChattanoogaFC.com

BUST OUT THE GRILL AND PUT ON THE GOLD AND BLUE
WHEN TAILGATING SEASON COMES AROUND IN CHATTANOOGA!

The University of Tennessee at Chattanooga takes its tailgating *very* seriously. Avid fans can rent a spot in the First Tennessee Pavilion across from Finley Stadium or find street parking near the stadium. For the fun of tailgating without all the work, come to the Mocs Block pregame party two hours before kickoff. Enjoy live music, concessions, and Scrappy's Kids Zone for the littlest fans. Grab a high five during the traditional Moc Walk, when the players make their way through the pavilion on their way to the stadium. Conclude the pre-game festivities by joining in the spirit parade, following the UTC marching band, cheerleaders, and dance teams into the stadium for the main event.

First Tennessee Pavilion
1829 Carter St.
GoMOCS.com

GATHER YOUR CREW
FOR THE HEAD OF THE HOOCH FALL REGATTA

Each year the Tennessee River is filled with nearly two thousand shells (boats) with ten thousand seats (people) competing in the Head of the Hooch. The unusual name comes from the Chattahoochee River, where the race originally took place. The popular regatta outgrew two venues before finding a home in Chattanooga, where it's one of the largest rowing regattas in the world. High school and college crews, as well as master rowers, race against the clock, with events launching from the starting line every fifteen seconds. Spectators can cheer the rowers at any point along the Riverpoint Park lining the three-mile course or on the downtown bridges, which provide a great roost above the races.

HeadofTheHooch.org

TAKE A TWIRL
AT ICE ON THE LANDING

When the weather turns cold, expect locals to start talking about two things: the blizzard of '93 and Ice on the Landing. Chattanoogans of all ages bundle up and head to the Chattanooga Choo Choo gardens (see page 92) to show off their best tricks. From November to January, a medium-sized outdoor ice skating rink is erected behind the Chattanooga Choo Choo hotel, along with risers for spectators. Novice skaters need not worry: Ice on the Landing provides "skate buddies," which are walkers with cut tennis balls on the back legs. It might seem silly, but they're handy for extra support on the ice and are preferable to taking a fall. Skate rentals and concessions are also available. Keep in mind that Ice on the Landing is a local favorite. Be prepared to skate in a crowd.

Chattanooga Choo Choo Hotel
1400 Market St.
IceOnTheLanding.com

TRAVEL TO THE NORTH POLE
VIA THE POLAR EXPRESS

All aboard the Polar Express! Every Christmas season the Chattanooga Railroad Museum transforms its Missionary Ridge Local line into the "North Pole Limited." Come in PJs and take a ride on the Polar Express. Enjoy snacks and sing carols while the train slowly passes by Christmas light displays along the tracks. The final stop is the North Pole, where Santa boards and gives each child a special gift to remember the ride. Just like in the book, the children receive a sleigh bell from Santa's sled to help them remember their special trip.

Chattanooga Railroad Museum
4119 Cromwell Rd.
TVRail.com

ADRENALINE JUNKIES, STASH YOUR GEAR
AT CHATTANOOGA'S UNOFFICIAL BASE CAMP, THE CRASH PAD

Hostels may have a reputation for stinky bedsheets and bedbugs, but the Crash Pad gives you the convenience and cleanliness of a downtown hotel at a fraction of the price. Not into communal bunking? Private rooms are available for a little higher price. The hostel is located in Southside, a short trek to the mountains, rivers, and trails begging to be explored. Need to unwind after a long day of thrill seeking? Head next door to the Flying Squirrel, where the exposed cedar beams and open-air concept make for a cozy, inviting atmosphere to kick back and relax. But don't leave without trying the Cuban tacos; your taste buds will thank you!

The Crash Pad
29 Johnson St., 423-648-8393
CrashPadChattanooga.com

Flying Squirrel
55 Johnson St., 423-602-5980
FlyingSquirrelbar.com

CRAWL THE WALLS
AT AN INDOOR CLIMBING GYM

Avoid the bugs, snakes, and inclement weather at one of Chattanooga's indoor climbing gyms. Great for every age and experience level, climbing gyms are a way to try out the sport in a controlled environment with expert help on hand. Learn the proper use of equipment under the watchful eye of a guide, and gain the confidence and skills required to take on the mountains and boulders surrounding Chattanooga. Climbing gyms are also great for regular climbers who may not need assistance while climbing but are looking to connect with a local climbing community and keep their skills sharp during the spring-summer off-season.

High Point Climbing Gym (Downtown)
219 Broad St.

High Point Climbing Gym (Riverside)
1007 Appling St.
HighPointClimbing.com

Tennessee Bouldering Authority
3804 St. Elmo Ave.
TBAGym.com

SLEEP IN THE CLOUDS
AT CLOUDLAND CANYON STATE PARK

Take a peaceful staycation getaway at Cloudland Canyon State Park, just across the border in Georgia. Pitch a tent and spend a few days exploring the winding trails, backcountry hiking, and two cascading waterfalls. The park provides a daily itinerary that includes guided hikes and stargazing, along with seasonal activities like the catfish rodeo and hayrides. For a less rugged stay in the great outdoors, try one of the park's many glamping (glamorous camping) options. Cabins and yurts provide modern conveniences, such as running water and electricity, as well as stunning views of the canyon. Be sure to bring along a Color Cloud Hammock for the perfect perch to kick back and relax with your head in the clouds.

Cloudland Canyon State Park
122 Cloudland Canyon Park Rd., Rising Fawn, GA
GAStateParks.org/CloudlandCanyon

ColorCloudHammocks.com

TAKE A SELF-GUIDED TOUR
WITH THE BIKE CHATTANOOGA TRANSIT SYSTEM

Did you know Chattanooga was the site of the first Coca-Cola bottling plant? Or that Jimmy Hoffa was convicted of tax fraud in the Joel W. Solomon courthouse downtown? Have you seen the oldest building in Chattanooga (now Urban Stack, built in 1870)? Discover these stories and more on a Cornerstones Inc. self-guided architectural tour. To get around the city faster, take advantage of the Bike Chattanooga transit system. The rental process is fairly easy to navigate, and riders must be over sixteen and have a credit card. The kiosks offer a cheap daily rate, but be sure to dock the bike every 60 minutes or expect hefty fees. Choose your own adventure! Download a map, chart a course, and soak up the hidden history of Chattanooga.

BikeChattanooga.com

Cornerstonesinc.org/walkingtour

TIP

Trek down Georgia Avenue to the Fireman's Fountain for a bit of weird Chattanooga history. Originally a fence enclosed the fountain to discourage pedestrians from lounging on the memorial. In an extreme overreaction, Chattanooga officials decided to import alligators to protect the monument. While the alligators succeeded in keeping loiterers away, they frequently escaped their enclosure and gallivanted around downtown. They were soon removed, but the legend of when alligators roamed the streets of Chattanooga lives on.

631 Georgia Ave.

FIND YOURSELF BETWEEN A ROCK AND A HARD PLACE,
GO BOULDERING

Locals say bouldering in Chattanooga is as easy as picking any backyard close to Signal Mountain. Known for the best sandstone bouldering in the country, the tri-state area offers a plethora of fields. Beginners should check out Stone Fort on Montlake Golf Course, known as "Little Rock City." Bring crash pads and make sure to have a little cash on hand for the climbing permit. This field is great for all ages and skill levels and has comprehensive guide books, but it gets crowded during the fall-winter peak season. For a more challenging climb, head to Rocktown. A much larger field means it's less crowded during peak season, but be sure to bring food and a guide book, as it's a fairly long hike to get to the field.

Stone Fort/Little Rock City
1875 Brow Lake Rd., Soddy-Daisy, TN

TIP

The cardinal rule of climbing in Chattanooga is "Leave no trace." To make sure private locations stay open to future climbers, please be respectful of the landowners' rules about pets/camping, keep noise levels down, and pick up all trash.

TAKE THE PLUNGE,
DIVE INTO ONE OF
CHATTANOOGA'S WATERFALLS

Hikers of every skill level can search out the cool, clear cascades, blue holes, and plunge pools hiding in the hills around the city. Before heading out, be prepared. Know the difficulty of the hike, determine whether permits are required, and make sure the water is safe for swimmers. All the pertinent information can be found on RootsRated.com, which also has pictures of the trails and hiking guides. The most magnificent local waterfall is Fall Creek Falls, whose 256-foot cascade makes it the tallest free-falling waterfall in the Southeast. The water remains fairly steady year-round, but for the most spectacular viewing, visit during the spring or after a big rain.

Fall Creek Falls
10821 Park Rd, Spencer, TN

EXPLORE MACLELLAN ISLAND,
IN THE HEART OF THE TENNESSEE RIVER

Maclellan Island sits nestled under the Veterans Bridge downtown, in the middle of the Tennessee River. Captivated by its beauty and rich history, conservationist Robert Maclellan purchased the island in the 1950s to protect it from commercial development. Today the eighteen-acre island serves as a wildlife refuge and nature preserve, home to great blue heron and osprey. Rent a kayak from L2 Outside and hike the Maclellan Sanctuary. Keep an eye out for the rain shadow desert at the heart of the island. The anomaly was created by the construction of the Veterans Bridge, which blocks the light and rain over a strip of the island. The rain shadow desert only adds to the intrigue of the preserve's beautiful landscape.

L2Outside.com
ChattanoogaAudubon.org

GET A DUCK'S-EYE VIEW
OF THE RIVER ON A CHATTANOOGA DUCK TOUR

Using repurposed amphibious trucks from World War II, the Chattanooga Ducks drive passengers from downtown Chattanooga directly into the Tennessee River, making quite a splash. After the initial plunge, settle in for a short relaxing ride. The open-air boats give you an up-close view of the bluffs, both sides of Chattanooga's riverfront, and Maclellan Island (see page 72), which sits underneath Veterans Bridge. The guides are entertaining and perhaps a little cheesy, as they share the history of the river and how it's changed over the last century. The Duck Tours provide a laid-back cruise along the downtown riverside and are great for families and passengers of all ages. Well-behaved youngsters may even find themselves steering the boat!

ChattanoogaDucks.com

HIT THE SLOPES
ANY TIME OF YEAR
ON CARDBOARD HILL

No snow? No problem! In Chattanooga, sledders don't have to wait for winter to hit the slopes. Inventive locals enjoy the all-weather sport of cardboard sledding, which is exactly what it sounds like. Simply flatten a large cardboard box and head to the North Shore's Renaissance Park. Dubbed "Cardboard Hill," the steep incline provides all the fun of sledding without getting cold. Already conquered Cardboard Hill? White Oak Park in Red Bank and Ross's Landing downtown are other great spots to take the plunge.

Renaissance Park
River St.

White Oak Park
798 Ben Miller Pkwy., Red Bank, TN

Ross's Landing
100 Riverfront Pkwy.

HAVE AN A-MAIZE-ING DAY
AT BLOWING SPRINGS FARM

Celebrate the long-awaited arrival of fall at Blowing Springs Farm. Wander in the ten-acre Enchanted Maize corn maze, but don't worry about getting lost. Even the worst navigator can find their way to the exit by following the clues left along the path. Take first place in the old-fashioned pedal car race, where endurance and calf strength are put to the test. Of course, no farm is complete without animals. Head to the Critter Corral to pet an alpaca, feed the ducks, and watch the miniature cows and horses graze. Whether you take a hayride around the pasture, pick out the perfect pumpkin from the patch, or simply sip hot cocoa and watch leaves fall, Blowing Springs Farm checks every box for the perfect fall day.

Blowing Springs Farm
271 Chattanooga Valley Rd., Flintstone, GA
BlowingSpringsFarm.com

ROLL WITH THE PUNCHES
WITH THE CHATTANOOGA ROLLER GIRLS

A little bit of creativity and a whole lot of tape can transform a convention center ballroom into a flat track roller derby, home of the Chattanooga Roller Girls. The bouts are action packed, with each team of five aggressively racing to score points and block opponents without landing in the penalty box. With nicknames like Goldie Knocks and Smackagawea, it would be easy to dismiss the derby as a joke, but these ladies aren't messing around. They play hard and fast and have attracted a dedicated local fanbase. Each bout has a theme, and the fans show their support by dressing up in costume. Feeling brave? Try the VIP Suicide Seats, but keep an eye out or you may end up with a roller girl in your lap.

ChattanoogaRollerGirls.com

TAKE A BIRD'S-EYE TOUR
OF THE CITY WITH LOOKOUT
MOUNTAIN HANG GLIDING

No training is necessary to take a tandem ride with an experienced pilot at Lookout Mountain Hang Gliding. Rather than jumping off the top of a mountain, the tandem trip starts in a field on the ground. The glider is pulled by a plane to heights of fifteen hundred or three thousand feet and then released to soar above the mountains and through the clouds. With an instructor at the helm, passengers are free to enjoy the breathtaking views and unsurpassed beauty of the landscape. Not a daredevil? Pack a picnic and (from the safety of the mountainside perch) watch trained gliders take the leap. Come at sunset and expect a spectacular show.

HangGlide.com

PICK A SIDE
AT THE BAYLOR/MCCALLIE GAME

The Baylor Red Raiders and McCallie Blue Tornadoes have been clashing on the football field since 1905. The Cross-River Rivalry is the longest-running high school football rivalry in Tennessee history. The matchup is the biggest game of the season for both schools. This isn't just another game; they're playing for glory. Before the big night, students produce over-the-top hype videos, host pep rallies around mountainous bonfires, and occasionally pull pranks on their opponents. On game day more than ten thousand students, alumni, family, and fans pour into Finley Stadium. The energy around the field is electric, and the crowd gets downright fanatical. If you're not sure who to root for, don't just sit on the sidelines! Pick a side, put on the colors, and join the rivalry.

Finley Stadium
1826 Carter St.

NO TRICKS, JUST TREATS
AT BOO AT THE ZOO

Each October the Chattanooga Zoo invites families to spend Halloween where the wild things are. At Boo at the Zoo, kids can trick-or-treat, get a picture with their favorite character, join a zoo-wide scavenger hunt, or try to take top prize in the annual costume contest. Once the sugar high sets in, let the kiddos jump it off in the bounce house or meander through the mystery maze. The highlight of Boo at the Zoo is seeing the resident animals. Pet a goat, take a camel ride, watch spider monkeys swing from branch to branch, or, for cuteness overload, visit the famed red panda exhibit. Join in the spooktacular fun, but be sure to get tickets early, as they tend to sell out.

Chattanooga Zoo
301 N. Holtzclaw Ave.
Chattzoo.org

FIND YOURSELF
UP A CREEK
AT AUDUBON ACRES

Don't get trapped indoors by the smothering heat of a Tennessee summer. Spend the day cooling off in the Southern Chickamauga Creek at Audubon Acres. The family-friendly waterway is ideal for tubing and swimmers of every skill level. Rent a canoe or a kayak and navigate the gentle rapids stretching thirty miles from Chattanooga to Ringgold. Plot the perfect course with maps on the Audubon's website, and be sure to check water conditions before heading out.

Chattanoogaaudubon.org/paddle-south-chickamauga-creek.html

PLAY WITH BUGS
AT THE RIVERPOINT PLAY TRAIL

Populated with large, insect-shaped playground equipment and informational posts, the Riverpoint Play Trail invites youngsters to relax in a spider's web, ride on a caterpillar's back, or make themselves at home inside a honeycomb. The play trail includes expansive mowed fields begging for cartwheels and Frisbees. Be sure to bring a bike! The trails connecting each playscape are an easy ride for even the smallest cyclists. Bathrooms, water fountains, and picnic pavilions are just outside the park, making the play trail the perfect place to spend a sunny day.

The Riverpoint entrance to the play trail is located at South Chickamauga Creek on Amnicola Highway at Lost Mound Drive.

CULTURE AND HISTORY

SPEND A DAY
UNDER THE SEA
AT THE TENNESSEE AQUARIUM

The Tennessee Aquarium is Chattanooga's most popular tourist attraction, drawing more than half a million visitors each year. The aquarium is divided into two buildings, with an interactive waterworks winding in between (see page 55). Get an up-close view of monster fish, watch otters play, and dip two fingers into a frigid pool to pet a sturgeon. In the Ocean Journey exhibit, visit the Secret Reef, where tiger sharks, sea turtles, and schools of colorful coral fish swim in perfect harmony. Come during a dive show and watch professional divers swim with sharks and answer audience questions. Try to touch a stingray, catch a butterfly, or sit back and enjoy the aquatic acrobatics of the penguins showing off their diving skills. The tickets are a bit pricey but well worth the experience.

1 Broad St., 800-262-0695
TNAqua.org

SEE HOW CHATTANOOGA
REVAMPED ITS REPUTATION
AT COOLIDGE PARK

In 1969 Walter Cronkite reported that Chattanooga's pollution levels had reached emergency proportions, making it "America's dirtiest city." At the time, factories lined downtown, pumping chemicals into the air and river. As the industrial boom declined and factories closed, Chattanooga was left with an ugly reputation and an even uglier waterfront. From this sordid history, the 21st Century Waterfront Plan emerged. The plan focused on cleaning up the river and turning the city into a top-notch tourist destination. Coolidge Park was just one of the major projects to transform the face and feeling of downtown. The thirteen acres of green space include an antique carousel, interactive fountains (see page 55), and stunning river views, making it a tranquil place to kick back, relax, and (now that it's pollution free) breathe easy.

Coolidge Park
150 River St.

TAKE A SHORTCUT
TO THE TOP OF LOOKOUT MOUNTAIN
ON THE INCLINE RAILWAY

Avoid the switchbacks and motion sickness of driving up Lookout Mountain, and hitch a ride on the Incline Railway. The trolley-style railcar takes it slow and steady, straight up the steepest grade of the mountain, providing panoramic views of the valley. The railway was originally constructed for tourists looking to avoid the four-hour horse and buggy ride to see Point Park Battlefield (see page 113) at the top of the mountain. Over the last century the railway has drawn tourists looking for stunning views of Chattanooga and an easy trip up the mountain.

Bottom
3917 St. Elmo Ave.
RideTheIncline.com

Top
827 East Brow Rd.
Lookout Mountain

FIND YOUR INSPIRATION
AT THE HUNTER MUSEUM
OF AMERICAN ART

For more than one hundred years, the Faxon-Hunter mansion has stood on the bluffs overlooking the Tennessee River. In the 1950s the mansion was donated to the city and converted to the Hunter Museum of American Art. As the Bluff View Art District (see page 2) grew around it, the museum expanded, adding two additional wings. Today the preserved mansion is nestled between a sleek modern wing and a glass atrium. The permanent collection spans from colonial pieces to modern art, with varied media, including blown glass, sculpture, pottery, and photography. The atrium provides stunning views of the river, surrounding mountains, and Chattanooga's North Shore, offering a peaceful place to contemplate the nature of art, and the art of nature.

See the permanent collection for free on Throwback Thursday, an event open to the community on the first Thursday of the month.

10 Bluff View, 423-267-0968
HunterMuseum.org

SEE WHAT ALL THE FUSS IS ABOUT.
SEE ROCK CITY!

Since 1935, barns all around the Southeast have beckoned passersby to "See Rock City." Rock City began as a meticulously planned personal garden and has grown into Lookout Mountain's most popular tourist destination. Follow the narrow stone trail as it crisscrosses along the mountaintop for almost a mile. Squeeze between the boulders and try not to lose your nerve on the 180-foot rope suspension bridge. The trail leads to a one-hundred-foot waterfall known as Lover's Leap, with an overlook that allows you to see into seven states. However, without a degree in cartography, only Georgia and Tennessee are actually discernible. For breathtaking views of Chattanooga's fall foliage, plan a trip in late September or October, when the weather is ideal and the trees will be at their peak beauty.

1400 Patten Rd., Lookout Mountain, GA, 800-854-0675
SeeRockCity.com

TIP
Bundle up and make Rock City a part of your holiday tradition. Come after sunset from November to December, when the Enchanted Garden is transformed into a luminary winter wonderland.

WHILE YOU'RE AT IT,
SEE RUBY FALLS TOO!

The discovery of Ruby Falls Cavern was an act of dumb luck by entrepreneur Leo Lambert. In 1928 Lambert began converting Lookout Mountain into a tourist destination, adding an elevator shaft through the center of the mountain to a cavern at its base. While drilling, Lambert's team hit a pocket of air, revealing a previously unknown passage. Lambert and a small team explored the cavern, discovering unusual limestone formations and a 145-foot underground waterfall. Today visitors can take an hour-long guided tour through the narrow path, squeezing through limestone formations and ducking under stalactites to the grand finale, the famous Ruby Falls. Bear in mind that the majesty of Ruby Falls depends entirely on rainfall; during drought seasons the waterfall can get down to a trickle.

1720 South Scenic Hwy., 423-821-2544
RubyFalls.com

THAT *IS*
THE CHATTANOOGA CHOO CHOO!

Chattanooga has been a hub for train enthusiasts since Glenn Miller first asked, "Pardon me, boy, is that the Chattanooga Choo Choo?" Terminal Station opened in the early 1900s, providing the first nonstop passenger service from Chattanooga to Cincinnati. The terminal operated through the 1960s, when improved air and car travel options rendered the railway obsolete. For decades the dilapidated building sat empty, until it was recognized as a national landmark and reimagined as the Chattanooga Choo Choo hotel. Today the grand lobby's ornate architecture, platform/track markers, and preserved ticket counters are a nod to the building's rich history. In the gardens behind the hotel, Pullman train cars have been converted into one-of-a-kind accommodations, allowing visitors to sleep in a train car without the fear of motion sickness.

1400 Market St., 423-266-5000
ChooChoo.com

BREAK ON THROUGH
TO THE OTHER SIDE ON A
CHATTANOOGA GHOST TOUR

An innocent man lynched on the Walnut Street Bridge (see page 97), a Confederate soldier doomed to roam the Chickamauga Battlefield (see page 112), and a murdered art lover waving from the windows of the Hunter Museum of American Art (see page 89) are just a few of the spine-tingling legends explored on a Chattanooga ghost tour. Explore the darker histories of Chattanooga, told in dramatic fashion on a nighttime walking tour of Chattanooga's best haunts.

57 E. 5th St., 423-800-5998
ChattanoogaGhostTours.com

HIKE THE HISTORIC
AND TRAGIC TRAIL OF TEARS

Ross's Landing was established as a trading post by John Ross, a Scots-Cherokee who settled there in 1816. When President Andrew Jackson signed the Indian Removal Act, Ross became the principal chief of the Cherokee Nation and an outspoken opponent of the law. In 1838 the Cherokee were driven from their homes during one of the harshest winters in Tennessee history, led by Chief Ross. Thousands died of exposure, hunger, and disease along what is commonly known as the Trail of Tears. Pristine parks, well-manicured paths, and beautiful monuments stand in stark contrast to the painful reality of what they commemorate. As you walk where they walked, consider what they lost: their homes, their heritage, their very lives.

Cherokee Removal Memorial Park
6630 Blythe Ferry Ln., Birchwood, TN
CherokeeRemoval.org

The Passage
100 Riverfront Pkwy.

Chattanooga Audubon Society
900 N. Sanctuary Rd., 423-892-1499

Red Clay Historic Park
1140 Red Clay Pk., Cleveland, TN, 423-478-0339

"We are stripped of every attribute of freedom and eligibility for legal self-defence. Our property may be plundered before our eyes; violence may be committed on our persons; even our lives may be taken away, and there is none to regard our complaints. We are denationalized; we are disfranchised. We are deprived of membership in the human family! We have neither land nor home, nor resting place that can be called our own."

—Chief John Ross in a letter to the Senate and House of Representatives

WALK 2,376 FEET ACROSS
TENNESSEE'S LONGEST PEDESTRIAN BRIDGE, THE WALNUT STREET BRIDGE

The Walnut Street Bridge, known by locals as the Walking Bridge, is an iconic part of the Chattanooga skyline. Built in 1890, the bridge was constructed to connect a segregated, predominantly white Chattanooga to its black workforce living across the river in Hill City (present-day North Shore). The bridge was closed to vehicles in 1978 and sat unused for a decade before it was recognized as a historic landmark. Rather than leaving the structure to rot, it was restored and converted into Tennessee's longest pedestrian bridge. Today the bridge is a bustling shortcut across the river for walkers and cyclists, a favorite of locals and tourists alike. Take the half-mile stroll and consider the century of history held within its wooden slats connecting a once-divided city.

1 Walnut St.

GET IMMERSED IN ART
AT THE 4 BRIDGES ARTS FESTIVAL

The Association for Visual Arts (AVA) invites world-class artists to hang their masterpieces at the annual 4 Bridges Arts Festival. Screening more than 700 applicants, 150 artists are carefully selected to display and sell their work. The media are varied, including painting, photography, jewelry, and ceramics. Spend a day perusing the artists' booths in the First Tennessee Pavilion. For a bit of extra fun, play judge and try to guess which artists will win best in show. Feeling inspired? Bring home a piece of original work and start your own art collection. The festival includes food, live music, and stimulating conversation that artistry at this level evokes.

First Tennessee Pavilion
1826 Reggie White Blvd.
AVArts.org

DO THE HOP
AT THE AVA GALLERY HOP

To get a taste of the local arts scene, check out the AVA Gallery Hop. Across the city, galleries open their doors to the public. Meet the artists and enjoy free refreshments while watching live demonstrations of their work. The event is free, with a printable map of the participating galleries at www.avarts.org/gallery-hop. A double-decker bus provides transportation to each gallery.

Photo credit: Nicole Manning, Show Me a Smile Photography

SKIP THE MUSEUM,
HEAD OUTSIDE TO
CHATTANOOGA'S PUBLIC ART

Art is for everyone. This simple but radical idea is at the heart of Chattanooga's Public Art Plan. A branch of the 21st Century Waterfront Project (see page 87), Public Art Chattanooga provides grants for community installations, bringing art out of museums and onto the streets. These pieces weren't made for gallery walls or to sit behind glass. They were designed to be touched, handled, climbed, and explored. They spark conversation, inspiration, and a sense of civic pride. Today there are more than fifty permanent installations scattered throughout Chattanooga's sidewalks, streets, buildings, and buses, making otherwise bland spaces beautiful and compelling. Art is for everyone, and in Chattanooga, art is everywhere.

For a map of the collection and artist information,
visit Chattanooga.gov/public-art/collections.

RELIVE ONE OF AMERICA'S MOST FAMOUS COURT CASES
AT THE SCOPES TRIAL PLAY & FESTIVAL

The *State of Tennessee v. John Thomas Scopes*—or, as it is more commonly known, the Scopes Monkey Trial—started a pivotal discussion in American education about teachers' rights, science, and religion. In 1925 Scopes was prosecuted for violating the Butler Act, which forbid the teaching of human evolution in a state-funded school. For a sweltering week in July, Clarence Darrow and William Jennings Bryan faced off in the first trial nationally broadcast on the radio. Ultimately, Scopes was found guilty and fined one hundred dollars, but the trial opened the door for the repeal of the Butler Act and sweeping changes in public education. Attend the annual Scopes Trial Play & Festival and watch the drama come to life in the very courthouse where the original trial took place.

Dayton Courthouse
1475 Market St., No. 102, Dayton, TN
Scopesfestival.com

LEARN THEIR STORIES
AT THE BESSIE SMITH CULTURAL CENTER

For more than twenty years, the Bessie Smith Cultural Center has preserved and promoted the history of Chattanooga. Beginning with African artifacts, the museum traces black history from pre-slavery to modern day. Interactive booths allow you to see how each generation lived in the face of slavery, the Civil War, and Jim Crow. Listen to the haunting melodies of Bessie Smith, the famed "Empress of Blues," who began her career singing and dancing on the streets surrounding the center that bears her name. Learn how a handful of Howard High School students, with courage and nonviolence, worked to desegregate the city. See the faces of the citizens who broke barriers in civil elections, education, music, sports, and the arts.

200 E. MLK Blvd., 423-266-8658
BessieSmithCC.org

JUST BUST A MOVE
ON THE NORTH SHORE DANCE STEPS

For an interactive and whimsical walk, grab a dance partner and head to Frazier Avenue. Keep your eyes peeled for the bronze dance steps embedded in the sidewalk. Follow the numbered steps and learn everything from the waltz to the hokey pokey.

PAY YOUR RESPECTS
AT THE CHATTANOOGA
NATIONAL CEMETERY

Spend Memorial Day at the Chattanooga National Cemetery honoring the men and women who gave their lives in service to their country. Patriotic music is played to a solemn backdrop of thousands of white stone grave markers lining the hills, a reminder of the ultimate sacrifice for freedom. Explore history through the monuments and placards throughout the 120-acre grounds. Keep an eye out for the distinctive Andrews' Raiders monument, honoring the first recipients of the medal of honor. During the Civil War, Union soldiers hijacked a Confederate train to destroy telegraph wires along the Western Atlantic Railroad line from Atlanta to Chattanooga. The raiders have been honored in books, movies, songs, and with a small replica of the train they stole marking their burial place.

1200 Bailey Ave.
cem.va.gov/cems/nchp/chattanooga.asp

RELEASE YOUR INNER CHILD
AT THE CREATIVE DISCOVERY MUSEUM

"Be quiet! Don't touch that! Behave!" That's what kids expect to hear in a museum, but the Creative Discovery Museum throws out all the rules. Children are invited to explore, climb, investigate, invent . . . even play on the roof! Every square inch inspires imagination. Scale the two-story webbed playground. Get splashed in the interactive waterworks while learning how water currents steer ships and generate power. Check out hands-on stations, designed to spark curiosity in every age and ability. Learn a bit about science, music, art, and nature, and maybe even try a few experiments. Even the adults can't help but let their inner child run wild at the Creative Discovery Museum.

321 Chestnut St., 423-756-2738
CDMFun.org

BASK IN THE GLOW
OF THE SILVER SCREEN AT THE CHATTANOOGA FILM FESTIVAL

The cinema art scene in Chattanooga has recently been bolstered by the growing acclaim of the Chattanooga Film Festival. For one weekend a year, the festival draws thousands of cinephiles to bask in the glory of the silver screen. Selections range from three-minute shorts to full-length feature films in a multitude of genres. Film fanatics can buy weekend passes to attend screenings, connect with filmmakers at panels and workshops, or attend special parties and events throughout the city. Casual moviegoers can pick from the dozens of films and buy a single ticket. The Chattanooga Film Festival has something for just about everyone. To get a full list of the screenings, visit ChattanoogaFilmFest.com.

HUNT AND GATHER
WITH EASTER AT COOLIDGE PARK

On Easter Sunday, Coolidge Park (see page 87) is overrun with one hundred thousand eggs for the annual Easter at Coolidge. Hunt may be too strong a word, though; it's really more of a grab. The park is divided in half, with corded areas sectioned by age group. The kids line up outside the appropriate zone until the rope drops, then rush to gather as many eggs as their baskets can carry. The plastic eggs contain candy, coupons, and small toys. After gathering eggs, warm up in the pavilion with free coffee and donuts from Julie Darling's (see page 17). Thousands bring along folding chairs for the open-air church service that concludes the festivities. Save the time and stress of hiding all those eggs this year and make Easter at Coolidge a new tradition.

Easter at Coolidge
150 River St.
EasterAtCoolidge.com

TIP
This year, skip the ham. Make a reservation for Easter brunch at the Back Inn Cafe. The à la carte menu includes seasonal small plates alongside the cafe's signature dishes and specially prepared breakfast classics.

411 E. 2nd St., 423-265-5033
BluffViewArtDistrict.com

STEP INTO THE CONFUSING AND COMPELLING MIND
OF HOWARD FINSTER AT PARADISE GARDEN

Reverend Howard Finster's otherworldly, self-taught pop/folk style won him acclaim in the art community and a faithful following. In 1961, before he found commercial success, Finster felt "compelled by God" to convert his backyard into a roadside attraction named Paradise Garden. For decades Finster transformed trash into shimmering mosaic walkways, religious monuments, and towering sculptures filling the three-acre garden. Known as a "man of visions," Finster considered his art sacred and himself a messenger of God. It's difficult to discern if Finster was an artistic genius, a hoarder, a little eccentric, or all of the above. In his life Finster created more than forty thousand numbered original pieces, but Paradise Garden remains his single greatest artistic accomplishment.

200 North Lewis St., Summerville, GA, 706-808-0800
ParadiseGardenFoundation.org

TOUR THE OLDEST
AND LARGEST BATTLEFIELDS IN THE WORLD AT CHICKAMAUGA BATTLEFIELD

In 1861 Tennessee was the last state to join the Confederate States of America, dividing our nation in two and starting a bloody civil war. Tennessee's defection was done over the strong objections of East Tennesseans, who unsuccessfully tried to secede from the secession. Chattanooga's central location and railway station made it an important stronghold, referred to as the "Gateway to the Deep South." When Chattanooga finally fell to the Union, one Confederate soldier famously called it the "death knell of the Confederacy." Learn about this dark chapter of American history on a tour of the Chickamauga and Chattanooga National Military Park. Walk the half dozen battlefields spread over nine thousand acres, the largest and oldest preserved battlefields in the world.

Chickamauga Battlefield
3370 Lafayette Rd., Fort Oglethorpe, GA
Nps.gov/chch/index.html

RETRACE THE PATHWAY
TO THE BATTLE ABOVE THE CLOUDS

The Civil War raged in and around Chattanooga. For months the Union gained ground, but they couldn't break the Confederate stronghold on Missionary Ridge. As a dense fog rolled in around Lookout Mountain, the Union soldiers used the cloud cover to scale its northwest side. The surprise attack upended the Confederate troops from their perch, forcing them to retreat farther into Georgia, giving control of Chattanooga to the North. This turn of events became known as the Battle above the Clouds, which is memorialized at Point Park. Take the steep hike from Cravens House to Sunset Rock, along the same incline Union soldiers trudged. Plan a hike in the evening for a spectacular panoramic view of the city as the sun sets.

Point Park Visitor Center
110 Point Park Rd., Lookout Mountain, TN, 423-821-7786
Rootsrated.com/chattanooga-tn/hiking/cravens-house-loop-rifle-pits-guild-hardy-gum-springs-bluff-trail

SHOPPING AND FASHION

GET LOST IN A GOOD BOOKSTORE
AT MCKAY'S BOOKS

Bookworms, audiophiles, video gamers, and comic book lovers: there's something for every enthusiast at McKay's Books. The two-story used bookstore is stocked with eighteen thousand square feet of books, DVDs, records, and more. Inventory changes daily, so every shopping experience is unique. Wide aisles and clearly labeled, well-organized shelves are designed for maximum browsing. If you want to save a little money on the trip, bring items to trade in. Double-check McKay's website, which lists what items they accept, but books, DVDs, video games, and records in good condition are a safe bet. Whether adding to a well-loved collection or discovering a new obsession, start at McKay's.

7734 Lee Hwy., 423-892-0067
McKayBooks.com

SAVE THE ELBOW GREASE,
GET PINTEREST PERFECT DECOR
AT VINTEREST

Remember that Pinterest project you pinned but never got around to creating? Head to Vinterest Antiques, where Pinterest is brought to life. The sixteen-thousand-square-foot warehouse is packed with more than one hundred vendors selling a healthy mix of vintage, antique, and the utterly unique. From rustic remakes to classics restored to their former glory, there's something for every style and aesthetic at Vinterest.

2105 Northpoint Blvd., Hixson, TN, 423-551-4790
VinterestAntiques.com

Southside
2121 Chestnut St. 423-498-4825

SHOP LOCAL, SHOP UNIQUE,
SHOP FRAZIER AVENUE

Spend Small Business Saturday shopping the eclectic, locally owned boutiques lining Frazier Avenue. Browse original artwork, secondhand books, vintage toys, charming housewares, and delicate handmade jewelry while supporting local businesses and artisans. Don't shop till you drop! Take a break and get re-caffeinated at Stone Cup Cafe. The second story of the coffeehouse is the perfect perch to rest and refuel. Kick back in the cozy chairs while enjoying an unobstructed and unparalleled view of the walking bridge and downtown Chattanooga. Once you get that second wind, check out the shops off the main drag on the backside of Frazier Avenue, surrounding Coolidge Park, and along the side streets of North Shore.

Stone Cup Cafe
208 Frazier Ave., 423-521-3977
StoneCupCafe.com

TIP

For a truly one-of-a-kind shopping experience, sift through the racks of Collective Clothing. This funky thrift store has everything from vintage cowboy boots to that thing you still can't believe you wore in high school.

40 Frazier Ave., 423-208-0940

GO WALKING IN A WINTER WONDERLAND
AT THE WAREHOUSE ROW HOLIDAY OPEN HOUSE

The Warehouse Row shopping plaza encompasses almost a full block of downtown Chattanooga. The gleaming hardwood, exposed brick, and warm, low lights hint at the building's previous life as a turn-of-the-century textile plant. Today, upscale boutiques, fine dining, and a luxury spa make Warehouse Row a one-stop shopping destination.

During the Christmas Season, Warehouse Row transforms into a twinkling wonderland. The annual Holiday Open House provides free appetizers, giveaways, live reindeer, and a dazzling tree. Best of all, attendees can get a free picture with Santa Claus! It can be a pretty long wait to meet Santa, so you better not pout, or you might end up on the naughty list.

Warehouse Row
1110 Market St.
WarehouseRow.com

TAKE IT EASY, EASY LIKE SUNDAY MORNING,
AT THE CHATTANOOGA MARKET

Where can shoppers buy fresh produce, support local artists, enjoy live music, and get their faces painted? At the Chattanooga Market, held every Sunday from April through December in the First Tennessee Pavilion. It includes special holiday celebrations for Mother's Day, Oktoberfest, Halloween, Thanksgiving, and Christmas. Inside, rows of vendor booths offer everything from handmade pottery to kettle corn. Many booths offer free samples of the goodies they sell, but don't fill up. Grab lunch at one of the food trucks in and around the pavilion. There's limited seating near the stage that tends to fill up quickly. Fortunately, the grass just outside the building makes a fine place to plop down for an impromptu picnic.

1829 Carter St.
ChattanoogaMarket.com

WORK UP A SWEAT
AT THE SIMS FAMILY FARM

Slather on some sunscreen and don't forget a cap; it's harvest time! The Sims Family Farm offers you-pick seasonal harvests, where fresh fruit enthusiasts can get their produce straight from the vine. Strawberries, blackberries, blueberries, and corn are available by season and purchased by the pound. Want to buy fresh local produce without all the work of picking? Check out the Chattanooga Market (see page 121) and farmers markets, held weekly around the city.

Sims Family Farm
1608 Burning Bush Rd., Ringgold, GA, 706-866-4062
SimsFamilyFarm.com

THE NORTH POLE
COMES TO NORTH SHORE DURING THE HOLIDAY OPEN HOUSE

Whoever said 'tis better to give than to receive obviously didn't do much Christmas shopping. Trying not to break the bank on a mother-in-law with expensive taste? Looking for a unique gift for that friend who eschews all things commercial? Searching for something fun for nephews and nieces who seem to own every single item in the toy catalog? Let's face it, it can be a bit of a nightmare. But the North Shore Merchants Collective Holiday Open House has got your back! Peruse the eclectic shops along Frazier Avenue (see page 118), offering special discounts and free holiday snacks. There are activities all weekend long, including a scavenger hunt and live music. Once everyone is checked off your list, reward yourself with a scoop of holiday cheer from Clumpies (see page 18).

Frazier Avenue
NorthPoleOnTheNorthshore.com

GAS UP THE TRUCK
AND TAKE A ROAD TRIP ALONG THE
WORLD'S LONGEST YARD SALE

Take the scenic route and haggle for the best deals at the World's Longest Yard Sale. Running along Highway 127 from Michigan through Chattanooga on its way down to Alabama, the sale stretches 690 miles and crosses six state lines. Held annually the first week of August, the World's Longest Yard Sale is a picker's dream. Shop along the two-lane highway, where vendors have set up tents and tables to sell collectibles, or follow yard sale signs off the beaten path. There's no telling what treasures await.

127sale.com

TIP

For the best shopping experience,
clear out the trunk, bring cash, drink
lots of water, and wear comfy shoes.

SUGGESTED
ITINERARIES

HEY THERE, SPORTS FANS!

SEE THE FALL FOLIAGE

· ·

HAVE A HOLLY JOLLY CHRISTMAS

FREE OR FAIRLY CHEAP

FUN FOR THE WHOLE FAMILY

NOT YOUR AVERAGE DATE NIGHT

TAKE A STEP BACK IN TIME

ACTIVITIES
BY SEASON

SPRING

SUMMER

• •

FALL

WINTER

INDEX